What people are saying...

"Beautiful and playful, Mamatee and Me Save the Sea, is an endearing story which helps children understand the impact plastic pollution has on our oceans! Beyond the adorable story, this book provides age-appropriate actionable steps for children to help solve the problem of plastic pollution and save our planet!"

Chance & Sarah Katherine Ruder, Founders of Last Chance Endeavors: an environmental education nonprofit

"Playful, informed, and inspired can't even sum up the feelings I experienced while reading this book. Through rhymes and storytelling, C.Chelle has masterfully crafted a book demonstrating human environmental impact. The science facts and pictures included in the book sum up what readers and Mamatee have in common: family."

Kelsey Anderson, video/audio producer for Meet the Ocean: an educational nonprofit developing dynamic programming for youth.

Mamatee and Me
Save the Sea

Illustrations by Brian Beausoleil

SUMMERS ISLAND PRESS
Thorne Bay, Alaska

ISBN: 978-1-957940-00-7

Published in the United States by

Summers Island Press
P.O. Box 19293
Thorne Bay, Alaska 99919

Website: www.SummersIslandPress.com

For information contact: info@SummersIslandPress.com

Summers Island Press is an imprint of the Wilderness School Institute, a nonprofit educational organization that offers outdoor youth activities for wilderness settings, including training in wilderness skills and nature studies, as well as the publication of curriculum on related subjects, through their Summers Island Press imprint.

Manatee photos by Chelsea Lauer and James Cotton from *SV Free Spirit*

Author photo by Shayne Sanders

Mamatee and Me Save the Sea / Hardback Edition

Dedicated to YOU and all the children of the future. Thank you for opening your heart and mind to a world beneath the waves. And for all that you will grow to be to protect our wonderful planet.

You will make a great light of difference in this world—and I can't wait to see what you become!

Come with me, Babytee.

We have much to do around the sea.

But Mamatee—what's there to do?
The sea is still so nice and blue.

And blue it shall be but...look, Babytee—a six pack ring! It will not let this dolphin sing!

Looks like the bottle won't let that shark swallow!

16

That's right—that's right–but watch
out for his bite!

Here's the sea turtle. Look—can you tell?
Her sense of smell can't work very well!

That has to be the last straw, right Mamatee?

Help! My mother is breathing slow—I think there is something wrong with her blow!

Mamatee, what could it be?

Let's have a look and we shall see.

Thank you, Mamatee! My blow is free!
Mamatee, this seems all wrong. Where in the sea do these things belong?

Somewhere on the surface, they must serve some purpose.

But they harm the sea. Is that right, Mamatee?

23

Mamatee! Mamatee!
What shall we do?
Nobody can help us—
not even you!

Yes, Babytee, it seems unfair but I promise you—somewhere—somebody cares!

It may be hard to understand—but look—
here they come to lend us a hand!

27

Thank you—thank you! Now we are free!

Will you help us keep our sea garbage free?

Ways to help Mamatee...

Notice a six-pack ring packaging your soda?

Try not to buy items packaged with six-pack rings, but if there are no other choices, cut them up before throwing them away.

This will help wildlife–like our dolphin friend–keep from getting tangled up.

Going out to eat?

"NO STRAW, PLEASE."

When you order your drink, remember to politely ask for no straw.

There are a lot of reusable choices out there.

Not only will you look cool, you will keep plastic straws out of our ocean!

You can choose!

And don't forget...

Helping your parents shop?

Remember to bring your reusable shopping bags to avoid adding more plastic trash to our oceans.

Mamatee and friends will THANK YOU!

Having a beach day?

Leave only footprints. Make sure you clean up after yourself.

If you see an item on the beach left by someone else, try to pick it up. It might not be a lot but a little goes a long way!

Pick things up!

Drinking water?

Use your reusable water bottle throughout the day to help keep plastic ones out of the ocean.

Use it again!

What **C.Chelle Cox** likes to do...

Ask your parents for permission to start a beach cleanup:

Invite your friends! Wear gloves (gardening gloves are a great way not to use the plastic throw-away kind).

Bring bags for trash pick up and sort items so they can be recycled or thrown away in the right place.

Celebrate your hard work with pictures and share the difference you made!

About

C.Chelle Cox

C. Chelle Cox grew up in the midwest.
There were fields of corn, but that did not suit her best.
As she grew she discovered a place called the sea.
Everyday she daydreamed of what it could be.
She went on adventures and learned how to dive.
Took pictures—wrote of moments she felt most alive.

She collected the best ones to put in a book, so, kids—just like you—
could have a good look. But wait. That's not all. There's more inside!
Something for kids to do far and wide.

You can help the sea without leaving your yard. It might take some
time (and could even be hard). The way to begin is by making a start.
Our sea can be saved if we all do our part!

That is what C.Chelle Cox has to say. If you want to help her...

You can start TODAY!

Hey, there, dive buddies—let's meet
The Manatees!

Manatees don't have any enemies. Yep, it is true. Sharks, alligators, crocodiles, and orcas could eat them— but they don't often share the same waters, so it is pretty rare. The manatee's biggest threat is humans.

Boat strikes, trash tangles and dirty water come from humans crowding into manatee territory. That's why it is so important we do our part to keep their home clean. And be careful when visiting, too.

They like to spend time in shallow water where it's warmer. That's also why there are such beautiful light patterns around them. Especially on clear days, like this one.

Manatees breathe through their noses, which they can close off when diving. That's how they keep the water out.

You can sometimes tell them apart by their different scars. The kind that come from running into boats. But they can be from getting tangled up in fishing gear, too.

Manatees eat sea grasses, weeds and algae–a LOT of it. The baby manatees drink their mothers' milk.

When they aren't munching, they are sleeping or playing. They are curious and friendly to humans but NO TOUCHING ALLOWED. That's the rule if you want to visit them where they live.

They can hold their breath for up to 20 minutes. Don't try it at home! They are great breath holders, but when they are active, they surface for air every 2-5 minutes.

Sleeping manatees will take naps on the bottom but will still have to surface for breath every few minutes.

Well, that's all for now, dive buddies. Thanks for coming along, with me. Remember to always be kind to our wild friends and I will see you next time!

The End

C.Chelle Cox

Courtney Michelle Cox

Children's Book Author:
Mamatee and Me Save the Sea

For more information & ways to purchase:
cchellestories.com

#MamateeAndMe

About the Author

Sailor, diver, children's book author, and multimedia creator, **Courtney Michelle Cox** has been driving boats ever since she could walk. Since then, she has sailed on a wide variety of maritime vessels, from center-consoles to tall ships, and motor yachts to small cruise passenger vessels. Currently, she works full time as an Assistant Expedition Leader for Lindblad National Geographic Expeditions. With them, she has helped lead trips as far south as the Panama Canal and north to Southeast Alaska. In 2019, Courtney received her PADI Divemaster on the world's second largest barrier reef off the coast of the small Honduran barrier island of Roatán.

When not busy at sea, Courtney likes to travel on her own adventures. She has been featured in *Coastal Angler Magazine,* interviewed legendary maritime archaeologist, Dr. James P. Delgado on his un-coverings diving the Titanic shipwreck, and been published in the prestigious *Venice Magazine* of Fort Lauderdale, Florida. She is also a freelancer for *Meet the Ocean,* where she helps produce entertaining and informative ocean content for their award-winning podcasts.

Mamatee and Me Save the Sea is her first children's book, in which she shares her passion for the conservation of this wonderful planet we all share. You can get in touch with her over at:

CchelleStories.com

Acknowledgements

Family

Nobody reaches their dreams entirely by themselves and I am thankful
to all the following for helping me with mine:

My Mom and Dad

I know my path in life is hard too keep up with and trying at times.
Thank you for allowing me to express myself and for teaching me to
chase passion above all. I am so lucky to have grown up with parents
who sacrificed so much to allow me to chase my dreams.

My brother Tanner

For inspiring me to stay driven and enjoy the drive.

Great Grandma Ruth Paoletti

For being the reason I was able to fall in love with the ocean as a child.

Grandma and Grandpa Griffith

For igniting my love and appreciation for all living things.

Nonni and Poppy

For giving me a space to grow into myself and never doubting my
direction in life.

Uncle Todd

For giving me my confidence at the helm at a young age and
for being one of my biggest fans.

Aunt Lynette

Your life is celebrated with every adventure I
have beneath the waves.

Friends

Schooner Freedom Charters

For teaching me to sail and giving me my sea legs.

The Cotton Family

For bringing my ocean dreams to life.

All my SEASTERS

For sharing salty adventures with me, loving me and
challenging me to explore new possibilities in this
great big blue world!

About the Illustrator

Work that is colorful and vibrant, with a certain storybook pleasure, **Brian Beausoleil** paints from the heart no matter what the subject is. He has a masters level in fine art and illustration, two years of study with a former Disney animator, and brings a great sense of joy and satisfaction to his work. He has been painting professionally for over thirty years, and also serves as a member of the board of directors for PRIMA, the Pacific Rim Institute of Marine Artists.

You can see more of his work and connect with him over at:

BrianBeausoleil.crevado.com

A Note to Readers...

Thank you for reading this book. If you enjoyed it, tell someone! Or consider leaving a review for it at any of your favorite online places. If you would like to read other books like this, you can find them by visiting:

SummersIslandPress.com

You will also find the Wilderness Kids Club over there. It's a place to learn about Nature and meet other kids who also like to spend time in the "Great Outdoors." There is even a real Wilderness Expert on hand who can answer any questions you might have about the wilderness and how to explore the pieces nearest to you.

A Note to Parents...

Summers Island Press and Wilderness Kids Club are divisions of the Wilderness School Institute, a nonprofit educational organization based in Alaska. They are dedicated to giving children something better to do, and bringing more hope and heroes into their lives. For more information, or to find out how you can become involved in some of their exciting projects, please visit:

WildernessSchoolInstitute.org

We take learning back to nature.

CPSIA information can be obtained
at www.ICGtesting.com
Printed in the USA
BVHW011000151222
654321BV00006B/337